CAMP COOKERY

LECTOR HOUSE PUBLIC DOMAIN WORKS

CAMP COOKERY

MARIA PARLOA

ISBN: 978-93-5344-869-1

Published: -

LECTOR HOUSE LLP
E-MAIL: lectorpublishing@gmail.com

CAMP COOKERY.
HOW TO LIVE IN CAMP.

BY

MISS M. PARLOA,

LECTURER ON SCIENCE OF COOKING, AND AUTHOR OF APPLEDORE
COOK BOOK, ETC.

CONTENTS

OUTFITS FOR CAMPING, AND HINTS FOR COMFORT.

THE first thing to parties bent on roughing it is the selection of a tent, which can be hired of any of the sail-makers, for any length of time, and at a reasonable price. For a party of seven or eight, an eight-foot wall-tent, is the best. Dig a trench around the outside to avoid nocturnal baptism the first time it rains. The beds can be comfortably arranged in the rear of the tent, by laying rubber blankets on the ground; on which lay boards slightly raised for the head, and sloping to the ground at the foot. These beds should be placed so that the persons will lie with their heads at the sides of the tent and feet toward the center. On the boards spread straw, hay, or dry seaweed, then the blankets. Every thing used about the bed should be laid in the sun every day. Some prefer sleeping on the ground rolled up in a blanket; but this is imprudent, except in very dry localities.

The next important thing is the stove. The top of a common cooking-stove with covers and stove-pipe to fit, which can be bought at any junk-shop for a trifle, serves very well in dry weather. Dig out a place in the side of a bank the size and shape of the stove-top, about two feet deep, and line three sides with brick or stones, with the front open. Regulate the draught by placing something in front for a blower.

"THE LEXINGTON CAMPING-STOVE," (which is the neatest, the most compact and convenient thing of the kind I ever saw), gotten up by the "Lexington Botanical Club" for their own use is just the article for camp. It is a box-stove, made of sheet iron, light, and quickly set up or taken down. It fits into a wooden chest which is thirty inches long, sixteen and a half deep, and fifteen broad. Into the stove fits a large water-tank; and, into the tank and one end of the stove, fit all the utensils for cooking and serving. When the stove is set up, the chest answers for a closet for stores, and also for a seat. This outfit is not prepared for the market by theorists who only guess at the wants of the camper, but has been studied out by gentlemen and ladies who, every year, spend months in the mountains, and who try to have all the comforts and conveniences possible, and yet to have very little baggage to transport from place to place. They have been using a similar stove for years; and we now have the result of continued improvements in the most perfect form of it. At my request, they have permitted their model to be used for the forming of others. They are made and for sale by J. A. Johnson, No. 5 Norfolk Place (opposite the Adams House). The whole cost of box, stove, and utensils will not exceed eighteen dollars.

Kerosene Oil Stoves are sometimes preferable, for they are easily transported, and can be used in wet or dry weather. The "Boston Gem," made by Francis Morandi, No. 102 Union Street, I find, after a thorough trial, works to a charm; the oven baking as well as my stove oven. The broiler is so made that there is no difficulty in broiling with it. When in the woods, if possible, I would have a good bed of coals for broiling.

In regard to Cooking Utensils, coffee and tea pots should not have spouts, but lips: and the lips should be riveted on. It is foolish for a party going any distance to try to carry crockery. Have tin plates and cups made, and they will last you for all your camping life. They can be kept clean by occasionally scouring them with sand if on the beach, and with ashes if in the mountains; or, what is still better, with Sapolio, which rub on a cloth and then rub the tin with the cloth. Four or six cakes of this will give you much comfort and neatness. If you can carry a farina kettle with you, and you use it with care, it will be almost invaluable to you, as by that means you can always be sure that your oat-meal, hominy, rice, &c., will always be cooked without burning. Always be sure that there is water enough in the bottom kettle.

Cleanliness.—It is very important that perfect cleanliness be observed in camp, as it adds much to health and comfort. When you pitch your tent, select a spot a little distance from it, for the refuse. Here dig a deep hole, if your stay is to be long, and into this hole throw the debris, each time covering with some of the earth which you have dug out. By this means you can keep the place clean and sweet.

Clothing.—Both ladies and gentlemen should dress in flannel throughout. One change of under-flannel is enough extra clothes to carry, but be sure to take plenty of stockings. Have your boots well made and with broad soles. For hats, broad-brimmed felt hats are the lightest and coolest.

Soap.—Carry plenty of soap for bathing, for washing dishes, and clothes. Take three or four pounds of baking soda with you to use for bathing purposes; and, if needed, for your mead and cooking.

Provisions for camp-life, will depend much upon the locality, and the requirements of the party; the following suggestions however, may be serviceable in making an outfit:—

When it can be obtained take Hecker's prepared flour, wheat, rye, Indian, or Graham. From this you will always be sure of good bread and griddle-cakes. Salt pork, smoked ham, bologna sausage, eggs, dried beef, salt fish. Game, fresh fish, and fresh meat are supposed to be obtained in the vicinity of camp. Pilot bread, crackers. Canned fruit and vegetables, where fresh cannot be obtained. Potatoes, beans, onions, Indian meal, molasses, sugar, salt, pepper, mustard, vinegar, butter, coffee, tea, chocolate, rice, oat-meal, baking soda, ginger, spice, soap, parafine candles, and kerosene oil.

The Essential Utensils are tin kettles with covers, coffee-pot, spiders with covers, gridiron, pans, basins, tin cups, pails, cans, knives, forks, spoons, lanterns, bags, ropes, strings, thread, needles, matches, shovel, axe, hammer, nails, slicking plaster, Jamaica ginger, fishing tackle, gun and ammunition, towels, stockings, and flannel garments. Each and every one of these articles may be found serviceable. The value of a match, a string, knife, a pin, or a pinch of salt, can never be realized, until in the woods or on the water the need of them has been felt. Parties scorning the idea of bothering with so many things when simply going out to *rough it*, will find it better to see that every thing is provided before starting; even then, they will find camp life rough enough.

CAMP COOKERY.

BIRDS.

In camp life, small and large birds should be either roasted, broiled, or stewed.

Pick all the feathers off, cut a slit in them, and draw them. Either wash or wipe carefully. If for roasting, tie the legs down, and place in the pan. Sprinkle with flour, cover the bottom of the pan with water, and roast, if ducks, thirty minutes, grouse and partridges the same.

Small birds, about half as long. The oven must be very hot.

Birds Roasted in their Feathers.

Open the bird in the usual manner, and draw it; then cover with wet clay, and bury in hot coals. In forty minutes, draw from the coals, and peel off the clay, when feathers and skin will come also.

A gentleman assures me that they are perfectly delicious cooked in this manner.

Broiled Birds.

Clean, and split down the back. Wipe dry, and broil over a clear fire, if small, ten minutes, but, if large, fifteen.

Season with salt, pepper, and butter, and serve on toast.

Stewed Partridges or Pigeons.

Place two partridges in a small kettle, and dredge with salt, pepper, flour, half teaspoonful of mace, half of cloves, and cover with cold water. Cover tight, and simmer two hours. Thicken with three spoonfuls of flour, and stir in two spoonfuls of catsup; simmer one hour longer, and serve. Grouse and pigeons are stewed in the same manner.

Brown Fricassee of Chicken.

Cut two chickens or old fowl into handsome pieces, and parboil them in just water enough to cover them; when they are tender, take them up, and drain them dry. Cut a pound of saltpork into slices, and fry them brown; take up the pork, dredge the chicken with salt, pepper, and flour, and fry a dark brown in the pork fat. When the chicken is all fried, stir into the remaining pork fat half a cup of dry flour; stir this until a dark brown, then pour on it one quart of the liquor in which the chicken was boiled. (This liquor must be boiling.) Season with pepper and salt to taste. Lay the chicken in this gravy, and simmer twenty minutes. Garnish the dish with boiled rice.

White Fricassee of Chicken.

Boil the chicken until tender, then cut it into small pieces. With the water in which it was boiled make a gravy, allowing half a cup of flour and two spoonfuls of butter to every quart of water. Season with pepper and salt; turn in the chicken, and let it boil five minutes, and serve. Garnish the dish with boiled rice.

Chicken Curry.

Make the same as white fricassee, with the addition of one teaspoonful of Indian curry to one pint of gravy, if it is liked strong, if not, half a teaspoonful. Dissolve the curry in a little water, and stir in. Garnish the dish with rice. Veal and mutton can be curried in the same manner.

Chicken Salad.

Boil tender four good-sized chickens; when cold, cut off the white meat, and chop rather coarse. Cut off the white part of the celery, and chop in the same manner. To two quarts and a pint of the chicken, allow one quart and a pint of the celery and a spoonful of salt. Mix well together, and then stir in part of the dressing. Shape the salad in a flat dish, and pour over the remainder of the dressing. Garnish with hard-boiled eggs, beets, and the tops of the celery.

Sauce for Birds.

Put one tablespoonful of butter into a pan; and, when it gets hot, add one tablespoonful of flour; stir until brown, then add one cup of boiling water, and salt and pepper to taste.

Broiled Chicken.

Split down the back, wash, and wipe dry, and broil over clear coals twenty-five minutes. Season with pepper, salt, and butter.

FISH.

Chowder.

Take either a cod or haddock; skin it, loosen the skin about the head, and draw it down towards the tail, when it will peel off easily. Then run your knife down the back close to the bone, which you take out. Cut your fish in small pieces, and wash in cold water. Put the head on to boil in about two quarts of water, and boil twenty minutes. For a fish weighing six pounds, pare and slice *thin* five good-sized potatoes, and one onion. Place a layer of potatoes and onion in the pot, then a layer of fish, dredge in a little salt, pepper, and flour. Keep putting in alternate layers of potatoes and fish until all is used. Use about one tablespoonful of salt, one teaspoonful of pepper, one teacup of flour in all.

Have ready half a pound of salt pork fried blown. Pour this over the mixture; add about two quarts of cold water, then strain on the water in which the head has been boiled. If this is not water enough to cover, add more cold. Cover tight, and boil gently thirty minutes. If not seasoned enough, add what you please. When it has boiled twenty minutes, put in six crackers which have been soaked three minutes in cold water. If you wish to add milk and butter, you can do so about five minutes before taking it up; but for my taste, it is much nicer and more natural without either.

Fish Chowder, No. 2.

Four pounds of fish, half cod and half haddock, if you can get the two kinds, two onions, six potatoes, eight white browns, one quarter of a pound of salt pork, salt, pepper. Prepare the chowder as directed in the preceding rule; split the crackers and lay on top, pour over the whole hot water enough to cover, and boil fifteen minutes; then wet two tablespoonfuls of flour with one third of a cup of cream. Stir this into the boiling chowder, let it boil up once, and serve. When you cannot get the white browns, pilot bread will answer. When a very strong flavor of onion is desired, use four onions. —*Mrs. T. Leighton.*

Fried Cod.

Cut the fish into squares, wash and wipe dry. Take half a cup of flour, half a cup of sifted Indian meal, and a tablespoonful of salt. Mix all these thoroughly. Dip the fish into the mixture. Have ready a frying-pan with *boiling* fat, half lard and half pork fat; drop in your fish. Fry a dark-brown on one side, then turn and fry the same on the other side, but be very careful not to let the fish or fat burn.

Have your dish hot, and lay your fish on it. Garnish the sides with the fried pork.

Broiled Cod, or Scrod.

Split, wash, and wipe dry a small cod. Rub the gridiron with a piece of fat pork, and lay the fish upon it, being careful to have the inside downward. If the fish is very thick, cook thirty minutes; but for an ordinary one, twenty minutes will be sufficient. Have the dish, in which you intend serving it, warm; place it upon the fish, and turn the dish and gridiron over simultaneously. If the fish sticks to the gridiron, loosen it gently with a knife. Have some butter warm, but *not melted*, with which to season it. Shake on a little pepper and salt, and send to the table.

Baked Cod.

Scrape and wash clean a cod weighing four or five pounds. Rub into it a heaping spoonful of salt. Make a dressing of three pounded crackers, a little chopped salt-pork about one teaspoonful of parsley, a little salt and pepper, and two tablespoonfuls of cold water. Stuff the belly with this, and fasten together with a skewer. Lay thin slices of pork on the fish, which should be placed on a tin sheet that will fit loosely into the baking-pan; dredge with flour. Pour into the pan about half a pint of cold water. Baste the fish often while cooking, with the water which is in the pan. If the water cooks away, add more, but do not have too much to begin with, or the fish will be boiled instead of being baked. Bake one hour. When the fish is cooked, turn the gravy into a bowl, then lift out the fish upon the tin sheet (from which you can easily slide it into the dish upon which you serve it); now turn your gravy into your baking-pan again, and place it on the fire; when it comes to a boil, thicken with a tablespoonful of flour, season with pepper and salt.

N. B. Always use a tin sheet in the baking-pan when cooking fish, as you then can preserve the shape.

Broiled Salt Fish.

Cut a square the size you desire, from the thickest part of the fish. Take off the skin, and wash clean; broil over clear coals ten minutes, then dip in boiling water, butter, and serve. This is a nice relish for breakfast or tea, and with boiled potatoes makes an excellent dinner.

Broiled Mackerel.

Split down the back, and clean. Be careful to scrape all the thin black skin from the inside. Wipe dry, and lay on the gridiron; broil on one side a nice brown, then turn, and brown the other side; it will not take so long to brown the side on which the skin is. (All fish should have the side on which the skin is, turned to the fire last, as the skin burns easily, and coals are not so hot after you have used them ten minutes.) Season with butter, pepper, and salt.

Fried Mackerel.

Fry brown six good-sized slices of pork. Prepare your mackerel as for broiling.

Take out your pork, sprinkle a little salt over the mackerel, then fry a nice brown. Serve the fried pork with it.

Baked Mackerel.

Prepare as for boiling. Make a dressing as for baked cod. Stuff with this; dredge with salt and flour. Bake thirty minutes, basting often with water, butter, and flour. Make a gravy with the water in the pan in which the fish is baked. Always make the gravy quite salt. The best way to cook mackerel is to *broil* it.

Smelts.

The only true way to cook smelts is to fry them, although they are sometimes baked. Open them at the gills. Draw each smelt separately between your finger and thumb, beginning at tail; this will press the insides out. (Some persons never take out the insides, but it should be done as much as to any other fish.) Wash them clean, and let them drain in a cullender; then salt, and roll in a mixture of half flour and half Indian meal. Have about two inches deep of boiling fat in the frying-pan (drippings, if you have them; if not, lard); into this drop the smelts, and fry brown. Do not put so many in that they will be crowded; if you do, they will not be crisp and brown.

Brook Trout.

Brook trout are cooked the same as smelts; or you can cook them as the angler does. They must be split nearly to the tail to clean. Wash and drain. For a dozen good sized trout, fry six slices of salt pork; when brown, take out the pork, and put in the trout. Fry a nice brown on all sides. Serve the pork with them.

Eels Fried.

Skin them; then turn on boiling water, and let them stand in it a few moments; then cut them into pieces about three inches long. Fry a nice brown, and serve.

Baked Eels.

Prepare as for frying; then put into a baking-pan, with a little water, flour, pepper, and salt. Bake twenty minutes. Make a gravy of the liquor in which they were baked, adding a little butter.

Boiled Halibut.

Pour into a pan about half an inch deep of boiling water; into this lay the side of the halibut on which is the black skin; let this stand a few minutes; then scrape with a knife, when the black will be found to peel off readily. Wash clean in cold water, then pin it in your fish cloth, and drop it into boiling water. For a piece weighing four pounds allow twenty-five minutes to boil. Serve with drawn butter.

Fried Halibut.

Take a slice of halibut, sprinkle with salt, and dredge with flour. Fry four slices of salt pork, add to the pork fat one spoonful of lard. When boiling hot put in the halibut. Fry a light brown on one side, then turn and fry the same on the other. Serve the pork with it.

Broiled Halibut.

Grease the gridiron with a little butter, place the halibut upon it, sprinkle a little salt over it, and place over clear coals. Cook one side ten minutes, then turn and cook upon the other side ten more. Have the dish warm; put the fish upon it, season with pepper and butter, and send to the table.

Smoked Halibut.

Broiled the same as the fresh, omitting the pepper and salt. Smoked salmon cooked in the same way.

Fried Salmon.

The same as halibut.

Broiled Salmon.

The same as halibut.

Salmon Trout.

When large enough, split down the back, clean and broil. Season with butter and salt. When small, open far enough to take out the insides; wash clean, and wipe dry. Fry the same as codfish.

Shad and Haddock.

Shad and haddock can be cooked the same as cod.

SHELL-FISH.

Clam-bake.

For a Party of from ten to twenty Persons.—First, make an oven of flat stones placed together in the form of a square, on a flat surface about two and a half feet square; around the edge of these, place other stones to form a bin. Fill this oven with small kindlings, such as can be gathered on the beach. On these, pile a few armfuls of larger sticks, crosswise, so that the top can be well covered with stones about the size of one's two hands. Start the fire, and allow it to burn down until the stones, which were on top of the wood, settle into the oven. Clean out all the cinders with a poker or stick; for, if allowed to remain, the smoke from them will spoil the bake. This must be done very quickly, that the oven may not cool Cover the oven with fresh seaweed about an inch and one-half thick. On the seaweed, spread the clams so the vegetables, &c., may be placed on top of them: then, in order, put on onions, sweet or Irish potatoes, or both, green corn, then the (blue or cod) fish, and a live lobster, if one can be had; if not, a boiled one, which will be very nice warmed up in this way.

Every thing to be used should be close at hand, to be put on the oven rapidly while it is very hot. Cover the whole bake with a piece of cheap cotton cloth, to keep out dirt; then cover all with seaweed until no steam escapes. Bake thirty-five minutes. Remove the covering from one corner at a time only,—so that the rest may keep hot,—and all hands fall to, and help themselves. It is nice eaten with drawn butter or vinegar and pepper.

To Prepare the Fish, Vegetables, &c.—A party of ten to twenty will require a bushel of clams, which should be washed in two or more waters (*fresh water;* salt water will not remove the fine sand); have ready, in a basket close at hand, as soon as the oven is hot. Clean the fish nicely, split the backs, season with salt and white pepper, and wrap in clean cloth. Peel onions, wash the potatoes clean, and cut the ends off; husk the corn, leaving the inner layer on to keep it clean.

Clam Chowder.

When intending to have clams in any form, get them in the shell if possible, the day before. Place them in a tub, and cover with clean water, and throw into this about a quart of Indian meal. This fattens them. When ready to use the clams, wash them thoroughly, then cover them with *boiling* water, and let them stand ten minutes, when they will open easily. Take them from the shell, cut off the black heads, and put the bodies of the clams in a clean dish. Strain the water in which they were scalded into the kettle in which you intend to cook your chowder. To one peck of clams allow three quarts of water. Let the water come to a boil, then thicken with half a cup flour which has been mixed with cold water, season with pepper and salt. Add the clams and a tablespoonful of butter; let it boil ten minutes. A few minutes before dishing, drop in three or four broken crackers.

Clam Chowder, No. 2.

For one peck of clams take six good-sized potatoes, pared and sliced thin, half an onion cut into pieces an inch square. Fry quarter of a pound of pork to a nice brown; place the pork and gravy, the potatoes and onions, in your kettle. Shake over the whole one tablespoonful of salt, two teaspoonfuls of pepper, and half a cup of flour. Strain over this four quarts of the water with which you scalded the clams. Place on the fire, and boil fifteen minutes, then add the clams and four split crackers; boil ten minutes longer, and serve.

Clam Boil.

Fill the pot with clams (which have been washed in a number of waters to remove all the sand); add hot water enough to get up a good steam, and boil until the shells begin to open; then serve.

Clam Fritters.

One egg, one pint of prepared flour, three-fourths of a pint of milk. Beat egg light. Stir milk into flour, then egg. Cut black heads from clams, mix with both, and fry in hot fat.

Scalloped Oysters.

Put a layer of oysters in an oval dish, and dredge in a little salt, pepper, and butter; then a layer of rolled cracker, and another of oysters; dredge the oysters as before, and cover with cracker; over the cracker grate a little nutmeg, and lay on small pieces of butter. Bake twenty minutes in a quick oven; add a glass of Madeira wine if you choose. Allow four crackers, two spoonfuls of butter, and one teaspoonful of pepper to one quart of oysters. Fill the dish to within an inch of the top.

Fried Oysters.

Drain the oysters on a sieve; roll them in cracker crumbs, and fry in *boiling* lard a light brown. Serve on brown-bread toast. When you desire them fried in batter, make one as for apple fritters, and fry in boiling lard. Have the dishes very hot.

Broiled Oysters.

Prepare in crumbs as for frying, and broil a light brown. Examine oysters carefully to see that there are not pieces of shell among them. Some oysters need more salt than others.

Oyster Stew.

Drain all the liquor from the oysters; put it into a porcelain kettle, and let it come to a boil; then skim off all the scum. Now turn in the milk, which you have let come to a boil in hot water. (Allow one quart of milk to one pint of oysters.) Stir in also one spoonful of butter or more, salt and pepper to taste. Now put in the oysters, let them boil up once, and serve with a dish of oyster crackers.

Oyster Soup.

Wash one quart of oysters, if they are solid, in one quart of cold water; if not, one pint of water; drain the water through a cullender into the soup-kettle; set the kettle on the fire, and when the liquor comes to a boil, skim it; then add one quart of rich new milk; just before it comes to a boil, turn in the oysters, and thicken with two spoonfuls of cornstarch wet with milk; then stir in half a cup of butter, and season with pepper and salt. Let this boil up once, and serve immediately. Be very careful that they do not burn. A safe way is to boil the milk in a basin, which is set into another of water, and then turn it on the oysters just before removing it from the fire.

Broiled Lobster.

Drop the live lobster into *boiling* water, and boil three minutes. Take up, drain, and crack the shell, but do not take out the meat. Lay on the gridiron, and boil slowly half an hour.

Serve in the shell.

To Boil Lobster.

Be sure that the lobster is living; if not, it is not fit for use. Have a kettle of *boiling* water; into this drop the lobster, and boil until the shell turns red. This takes about a half-hour. Take up; and when cold it is fit to eat.

Stewed Lobster.

Take out all the meat from the shell. Chop it, but not fine. Put into a basin with a little salt, pepper, butter, and half a cup of water to a small lobster. Stew about ten minutes.

Curried Lobster.

Prepare the lobster as for stew; when it comes to a boil, add a mixture of a heaping tablespoonful of flour, and half a teaspoonful of Indian curry mixed with cold water. Let this boil eight minutes, then serve.

Lobster Salad.

Lobster salad is made the same as chicken, using lobster instead of chicken, and lettuce instead of celery.

EGGS.

Poached Eggs.

Break and beat up two eggs, and stir into them two tablespoonfuls of milk and half a teaspoonful of salt; put them into a basin, with half a spoonful of butter, and set over the fire. Stir until it thickens, and then serve.

Scrambled Eggs.

Beat together four eggs, and then turn into a pan with one spoonful of melted butter. Stir quickly over a hot fire one minute, and serve.

Omelets.

Beat lightly two eggs, and stir in one spoonful of milk and a pinch of salt. Heat the omelet pan hot, and then put in a little bit of butter, and when melted turn in the beaten eggs; set on the fire, shake the pan, cook until a light brown; then fold the omelet and serve on a hot dish. Ham, mushroom, lobster, chicken, and all kinds of omelets are made by chopping up the meat, and laying it between the folds before dishing.

MEATS.

Fried Salt Pork.

Cᴜᴛ salt pork into slices a quarter of an inch thick, cut off the rind, and then pour over them boiling water, in which let them stand ten minutes; then turn off the water, and fry until they are brown on both sides.

Broiled Salt Pork.

Prepare as for fried, and broil ten minutes over clear coals.

Salt Pork Fried in Batter.

Fry the pork as before directed; dip in batter, and fry in the pork fat, to which should be added two spoonfuls of drippings or lard. Make the batter in the following manner: Mix gradually with one cup of flour one cup of milk, and then add one well beaten egg and a little salt.

Fried Ham.

Cut the ham in very thin slices, and cut off the rind. Have half a spoonful of boiling drippings in the frying-pan, lay the ham in this, and fry quickly eight minutes; it will then be brown and crisp. Where the ham is for dinner, have the slices larger and thicker, and if you do not have eggs with it, fry bread, as directed for sausages.

Broiled Ham.

Cut the ham in thin slices; cut off the rind, and broil over clear coals ten minutes. Butter or not, as you please. When the ham is very salt or hard, slice, and let stand in boiling water ten minutes before frying or broiling.

Ham and Eggs.

Fry the ham as before directed, and when the ham is all fried, turn the fat into a basin, and scrape the salt from the frying-pan; turn back the fat, and add to it half a cup of lard. When this comes to a boil, break in your eggs, leaving room to turn them, if you prefer them turned; they look much nicer, however, when they are not turned. If they are not turned, dip up the boiling fat while they are cooking and pour over them; they will cook rare in two minutes, well done in three. Lay them on the slices of ham, and serve.

Breakfast Bacon.

Cooked the same as ham.

Beefsteak Smothered in Onions.

Fry brown four slices of salt pork; when brown take out the pork, and put in six onions sliced thin. Fry about ten minutes, stirring all the while; then take out all except a thin layer, and upon this lay a slice of steak, then a layer of onions, then steak, and cover thick with onions. Dredge each layer with pepper, salt and flour. Pour over this one cupful of boiling water, and cover tight. Simmer half an hour. When you dish, place the steak in the centre of the dish, and heap the onions around it. Serve the same vegetables as for broiled steak.

Broiled Beef Steak.

Cut the steak about three quarters of an inch thick. Have a clear fire and lay the steak on the gridiron, and dredge lightly with flour. If you desire the steak rare, cook ten minutes, if well done, fifteen. Dish and season with butter, pepper, and salt. Serve *immediately*. Never set steak into the oven to keep warm or to melt the butter. The dish must be hot, the butter stand in a warm room long enough to soften, but do not *melt*. If for dinner, serve potatoes, either baked or boiled, and any other vegetables which you choose. Many persons pound tough steak before cooking, but I would not recommend it, as by this means it loses much of its juiciness.

There are some families in the country who have no means of broiling. The next best thing such persons can do is to heat the frying pan very hot, and grease with just enough butter to prevent the steak from sticking; then lay the steak in, and cook, and serve as before directed.

Fried Beefsteak.

For two pounds of steak fry brown four slices of salt pork, then take up the pork and fry the steak in the fat; salt and pepper it. When you dish, add a little butter. To the fat remaining in the frying-pan, after the steak has been cooked, add one tablespoonful of *dry* flour (be sure to have the fat boiling), and stir until it is brown and there are no lumps, then pour in about half a cup of boiling water. Season well with pepper and salt. Serve in a gravy tureen. This is a more economical, but not so healthy a method as broiling.

Stewed Beef.

Take a piece of beef that is rather tough or pieces of tough beefsteak; rub into it a handful of salt, some pepper and flour; lay in a kettle that you can cover tight, and that has a flat bottom. Cut up an onion, a potato, a *small* turnip, a carrot, and a parsnip; lay these on top of the meat, and then sprinkle in half a teaspoonful of cinnamon, half of mace, one-fourth of clove, and add cold water enough to cover it. Let them come to a boil, skim off all the scum; then cover tight, and simmer five hours. After it has been boiling four hours, mix half a cup of flour with cold water and add to it. You can then taste it, and add more seasoning if necessary. The spice may be omitted if you choose.

Lamb Chops.

Broil fifteen minutes over clear coals. Season with butter, pepper, and salt.

Broiled Veal.

Cut veal into thin slices, and broil twenty minutes. Season with butter, pepper, and salt. This is the most unsavory method of cooking veal, and I would not recommend it.

Fricassee of Veal.

Fry eight slices of salt pork, brown. Take out the pork, and put in *thin* slices of veal, which have been cut from the leg. Sprinkle with salt and pepper, and fry *brown*. When all the veal is fried, mix with the boiling fat two tablespoonfuls of *dry* flour; stir until there are no lumps, and the flour is brown; then add two cups of boiling water, and season with salt and pepper. Lay the veal in this gravy, and simmer fifteen minutes. Dish, and pour the gravy over the meat. If for dinner, garnish with boiled rice, and serve plain boiled potatoes.

Mutton Chops.

Cut the chops from the loin or the neck; broil as you do beefsteak, and serve in *hot* dishes.

Mutton Pie with Tomatoes.

Pare and slice six tomatoes; put a layer into a deep pudding-dish, then put in a layer of slices of cold mutton, and dredge in flour, salt, pepper. Have the last layer tomatoes, over which sprinkle two rolled crackers. Bake one hour.

Veal Cutlets.

Fry brown eight slices of salt pork. Take them up, and add to the fat two large spoonfuls of lard or drippings. Have ready thin slices of veal (they are best cut from the leg), dip them in an egg which has been well beaten, then into cracker crumbs, and fry a nice brown. Season them, before dipping in the egg and cracker, with pepper and salt. Serve with the salt pork.

Mutton Cutlets.

The same as veal.

Fried Sausages.

Cut the sausages apart, and wash; then lay them in the pan, and pour boiling water over them; let them boil two minutes, then turn off the water, and prick the sausages with a fork, or they will burst open when they begin to fry. Put a little drippings in the pan with them, and fry twenty minutes. Turn them often that they may be brown on all sides. Cut stale bread into fanciful shape, fry in the sausage fat, and garnish the dish with it. Brown bread is delicious fried in this way. Serve plain boiled potatoes.

VEGETABLES.

Boiled Potatoes.

If the potatoes are new, wash clean, and put into boiling water; boil thirty minutes, and serve immediately. As they grow older, scrape the skin off before boiling. For old potatoes, have a sharp knife with a *thin* blade; and pare the potatoes, having the skin as thin as possible. They are very much better if they stand in cold water a few hours before boiling; then put them in boiling water, and boil thirty minutes. When they have boiled fifteen minutes, throw in a handful of salt. When done, turn off the water, and let them stand on the back part of the range three minutes; then, shake them up once, and turn into the dish, and send to the table.

Baked Potatoes.

Be very particular to wash every part of the potato clean, as many persons eat the skin. Put them in a pan (have an old one for this purpose), and bake in a moderate oven fifty minutes. There is such a difference in ovens, that each one must learn for herself what the time will be for each; for some will bake in less time, and some will take much longer than the time designated.

Fried Potatoes.

Pare and slice *thin* raw potatoes, and let them stand in cold water several hours; if in summer, put a piece of ice in the water. Cut the slices *lengthwise* of the potato. Have ready a basin with *boiling* drippings or lard, drain the potatoes a minute in a cullender, and drop them into the boiling fat, and fry a light brown; take them out with a skimmer, and lay them in a dry cullender, which should be placed in a tin pan, and set in an open oven. There should be as much fat as for frying doughnuts, and there should not be any more potatoes put in at a time than will fry brown and not stick together. Have the basin in which you fry quite deep, as there is danger of the fat boiling over when the potatoes are put in. When you take the potatoes up, dredge a little salt over them. When potatoes are cooked in this manner, they will be light and crisp. If they do not get cooked enough at first, they are very much improved by dropping them into the fat for one minute, after they have been standing in the oven a while.

Fried Boiled Potatoes.

Cut the potatoes into slices, and fry in either pork fat or nice drippings. Have just fat enough in the pan to prevent their sticking, and sprinkle with salt while cooking. When these are brown, take them up and put in a little more fat, and fry as before.

Potatoes warmed with Pork.

Cut about eight slices of pork into pieces about half an inch square, and fry a nice brown. Have ready one dozen cold potatoes cut into slices, and turn them into the pan with the fried pork, and dredge in a little salt and pepper, then stir and cut them into small pieces with the knife. When a light brown, serve.

Potatoes warmed in Gravy.

Slice cold potatoes as for frying, and turn them into the frying-pan, and to a dozen potatoes add a pint of cold gravy. Season with pepper and salt, and stir, and cut with a knife, until they are hot and in small pieces.

Fricassee of Potatoes.

Cut cold boiled potatoes into small squares, and put them in a basin with milk, pepper, and salt, allowing half a pint of milk to a dozen potatoes. Set the basin into another of hot water, and when it comes to a boil, add a tablespoonful of butter, and set on the stove, and let it boil up once, then serve.

Boiled Sweet Potatoes.

Wash and boil, with the skins on, forty-five minutes. They are much better baked than boiled, and I would cook them so generally.

Baked Sweet Potatoes.

Wash and wipe dry, and bake one hour. Do not cook squash when you have sweet potatoes.

Boiled Onions.

When new and tender, they will boil in one hour; but after the month of October, they will require two hours. Put them into water before peeling them, and they will not affect the eyes. Peel off all the dark skin, and put them in hot water, and boil as directed. If you have milk plenty, half an hour before they are done, turn a quart into the water in which they are boiling. This makes them white, and is said to prevent in a measure, the disagreeable odor which always follows their being eaten. Boil them in a porcelain kettle. Dish them whole, and season with a little pepper, salt, and butter.

Fried Onions.

Peel and slice thin ten good-sized onions, and put them in a frying-pan with two spoonfuls of drippings. Fry thirty minutes, turning often.

Baked Squash.

Cut the squash in two, take out all the soft, stringy part; if you need the whole squash for dinner, lay the halves together, and put in a baking-pan (the old one you use for baking potatoes in), and bake forty-five minutes. When done, scrape the squash from the shell, and season, and serve as boiled squash. When you cook but half a squash, lay it with the inside downward. This is a nice way to cook watery squash.

Beets.

Wash clean, but do not scrape; if you do they will look white when cooked. When young they will cook in two hours; but old ones will require four or five hours. When done, plunge them into cold water, and the skin will peel off easily. Cut in thin slices.

Pickled Beets.

Cut the beets that are left from dinner into thin slices, and lay them in an earthen vessel, and cover with cold vinegar.

Shelled Beans.

Wash in several waters, and put them in a basin with boiling water. Boil one hour. Do not drain them very dry. Season with butter and salt.

Boston Baked Beans.

Examine and wash one quart of dry beans (the pea bean is the best), and put them in a pan with six quarts of cold water; let them soak in this over night. In the morning wash them in another water, and place them on the fire with six quarts of cold water and a pound of mixed salt pork. If they are the present year's beans, they will cook enough in half an hour; if older, one hour. Drain them and put half in the bean-pot; then gash the pork, and put in the remainder of the beans, one tablespoonful of molasses, and one of salt, and cover with boiling water. Bake ten hours. Watch them carefully, and do not let them cook dry.

N. B. As the water cooks away, add more.

String Beans.

String and cut into pieces about an inch long; then wash and put into boiling water, and boil one hour. Season with salt and butter.

Green Peas.

Put them into boiling water, and when very young they will cook in twenty minutes; but generally they require thirty. Season with salt and butter.

Boiled Rice.

Wash and pick all the specks from a cup of rice. Let it stand in cold water two hours, and then put it in a deep kettle, with two quarts of water, and boil *fast* thirty minutes. When it has boiled twenty minutes, throw in a great spoonful of salt. When done, turn into a cullender, and set in the oven a few minutes. When ready to dish, shake lightly and *turn* into the vegetable dish. Never use a spoon. If these directions are followed, you will have a handsome and healthy vegetable, and every kernel will be separate. The water in which the rice has been boiled makes a nice starch for colored clothes.

The Southern rice cooks much quicker and is nicer than the Indian rice. If possible, always purchase the former.

Boiled Rice, No. 2.

Wash one cupful of rice and put into a tin basin or pail, with three cupfuls of cold water, and a teaspoonful of salt, cover and set in another basin, with hot water, place on the fire, and boil thirty minutes. Rice is very healthy, and should be a common dish on the table.

Boiled Macaroni.

Break up and wash a pint bowl full of macaroni, and put in a shallow basin, and cover with cold water. Set this basin into another of warm water, and place on the fire; after fifteen minutes, add a pint of milk, and a teaspoonful of salt; let it cook ten minutes longer, then add a spoonful of butter, and cook five minutes more, and dish. Be careful not to break the macaroni in dishing. The boiled macaroni which remains from one dinner can be used for the next, by preparing it in the following manner: Butter a shallow dish, and turn the macaroni into it; then grate over it old cheese, and brown.

Boiled Green Corn.

Boil twenty-five minutes, if very young and tender. As it grows older it requires a longer time. Send to the table in a napkin.

Boiled Turnips.

Peel and cut into slices. If they are to be served in slices, boil with a small piece of pork. Boil the pork three hours, and put in the turnips; if they are the white turnip, they will cook in forty-five minutes; but if the yellow, they will require two hours. Serve in slices without any seasoning except what they get by being boiled with the pork.

Stewed Tomatoes.

Pour boiling water over half a peck of ripe tomatoes. Let them stand in it five minutes, and then peel off the skins; cut them into slices, and put in a stew-pan with a little salt, pepper, and a spoonful of sugar. Simmer two hours, stirring often to prevent burning. Two minutes before dishing stir in one tablespoonful of butter. Canned tomatoes are cooked in the same manner, but do not require more than half an hour to stew.

Sliced Tomatoes.

Pour boiling water over them, and then peel and slice thin; lay them on small platters, and serve. Let each person season to his own taste.

Baked Tomatoes.

Scald and peel as directed; have ready a dish, into which lay a layer of tomatoes (whole), then sprinkle with salt, pepper, and cracker crumbs; then another layer of tomatoes, and sprinkle again with salt and pepper. Cut a spoonful of butter into small pieces and lay on the tomatoes, and then cover with cracker crumbs. Bake thirty minutes.

Mock Bisque Soup.—Very nice.

Stew one can of tomatoes (one quart can). While the tomatoes are stewing, put three pints of milk on to boil, setting the basin in which the milk is into another of hot water. When the milk comes to a boil, stir in a tablespoonful of flour, which has been thoroughly mixed with a little cold milk. Let this boil ten minutes, and then add butter the size of an egg, salt and pepper to taste. The tomatoes, which were put on at the same time with the milk, are now ready to strain into the mixture. Just before straining, stir a pinch of saleratus into the tomatoes to remove the acidity. Serve immediately.

BREAD.

Corn Dodgers.

Take three teacups of Indian meal, one teaspoonful of salt, one tablespoonful of sugar, and pour on boiling water enough to wet it, nearly one quart; then make into small, flat cakes about an inch thick, and fry in *boiling* fat until brown. They will fry in fifteen or twenty minutes. To be eaten *very hot.*

Baked Corn Cake.

Three teacups of Indian meal, one teaspoonful of salt, one tablespoonful of sugar, one of butter; wet this with *boiling* water, and then beat in one egg. Spread half an inch deep on buttered tin sheets, and bake brown in a quick oven. This is delicious.

Oat-meal.

Oatmeal, Indian meal, and hominy all require two things to make them perfect; that is, *plenty of water* when first put on to boil, and a *long* time to boil.

Have about two quarts of boiling water in a large stewpan, and into it stir one cup of oatmeal, which you have already wet with cold water; boil this an hour, stirring often, and then add half a spoonful of salt, and boil an hour longer. If it should get too stiff, add more boiling water; or, if too thin, boil a little longer. You cannot boil it too much.

The only trouble there is in cooking oatmeal is, that it takes a long time; and surely no one will let that stand in the way when it is so much better for having the extra time. It is also very necessary that there be an abundance of water to begin with; if not, it will never be as good, no matter how much may be added after it has been cooking any time.

Hominy.

Wash in two waters one cup of hominy, then stir it into one quart of boiling water with a little salt, and boil from thirty to sixty minutes. It is better boiled sixty than thirty. Be careful that it does not burn. Hominy can be used more than oatmeal, as it can be eaten with any kind of meat, and should be cooked once a day. It is nice and appropriate for any meal. It is also good eaten warm or cold with milk.

Hominy Griddle-cakes.

To one pint of warm, boiled hominy, add a pint of milk or water, and one pint of flour. Beat up two or three eggs, and stir them into the batter with a little salt. Fry as any other griddle-cake. They are delicious.

Fried Mush.

Into two quarts of boiling water stir one tablespoonful of salt, and one cup of flour mixed with one quart of Indian meal (it may take a little more than a quart of meal to make it stiff enough); beat it well, or it will be lumpy. Boil gently two hours, and then turn into dishes which have been dipped in cold water, and set away to cool. Pans in which you bake loaves of bread are the best to cool it in, as it then makes handsome slices. In the morning cut into slices an inch thick, and fry brown in pork fat. Serve slices of fried pork with it. You can cook enough at one time for several breakfasts. If you do not wish to fry the mush, do not use the flour, and do not make quite so stiff.

Spider-Cakes.

Heat the frypan hot; also a cover for it. While heating, mix with one pint of Hecker's prepared flour half a pint of milk or water; grease the hot pan with pork, lard, or butter, and pour half the mixture into it. Make smooth with the spoon; cover, and cook four minutes; turn the cake, and cook four minutes longer. Take up, grease the pan again, and put in the remainder of the mixture, which cook as before.

Biscuit.

One quart of Hecker's prepared flour, one small pint of milk or water. Grease the pans, and drop the mixture by the spoonful on to it; bake in a quick oven from ten to twelve minutes.

N. B. If you prefer, shape into cakes with the hands.

Hecker's Prepared Graham.

Rye and Indian are nice to take into camp, as all that is necessary is to wet with milk or water, and bake. The buckwheat is nice also.

When you have Hecker's prepared Graham, rye, or Indian, use one half a cup of sugar to the quart of the preparation.

Milk Toast.

Put one quart of milk in a tin pail or basin, and set into a kettle of boiling water. When it comes to a boil, stir in two spoonfuls of flour, mixed with half a cup of milk, one spoonful of butter, and salt to taste; let this boil ten minutes, and then put in the bread, which must be toasted brown. Cook five minutes longer, and serve.

PUDDINGS.

Boiled Rice.

PICK and wash clean one cupful of rice, and put into a basin with a pint and a half of cold water; set on the stove where it will cook slowly; or, better still, set into another basin of water, and cook slowly. When the rice has absorbed all the water, turn on it one quart of new milk, and stir in one tablespoonful of salt; let this cook two hours, stirring often. Serve with sugar and cream.

Baked Rice.

Pick and wash one cup of rice; put it in a dish that will hold two quarts and a pint, and cover with fresh milk; stir into this two teaspoonfuls of salt, one table-spoonful of cinnamon, and four of sugar. Set this in the oven, and stir once in every half-hour; after it has been baking two hours stir in milk enough to fill the dish, and bake one hour longer (the dish should be nearly full of milk at first). Serve with sugar and milk.

Minute Pudding.

One pint of milk, one of water, nine tablespoonfuls of flour, one teaspoonful of salt, two eggs. Set the milk into a basin of hot water, and when it comes to a boil add to it one pint of boiling water. Have ready the flour, made into a smooth paste with one cup of milk, and mix with this paste, after they are well beaten, the two eggs; now take the basin in which the milk and water are, and set upon the fire; let it boil up once, and then stir in the thickening; beat it well, that it may be smooth, and cook three minutes longer. Serve with vinegar sauce.

Apple Dowdy.

Pare and quarter about one dozen good tart apples, put them in a kettle with one cup of molasses, a small piece of butter, and one pint of hot water. Set this on the fire, and let it come to a boil, and while it is heating make a paste with one pint of prepared flour and one half a pint of milk. Roll this out large enough to cover the apple, put it into the kettle, cover tight, and boil gently twenty minutes.

Down East Pudding.

One pint of molasses, one quart of flour, one tablespoonful of salt, one tea-spoonful of soda, three pints of blackberries. Boil three hours, and serve with sauce made in the following manner:—

One teacup of powdered sugar, one-half of butter, one egg, two teaspoonfuls of *boiling* water, and one of brandy. Beat the butter to a cream, and then add very gradually the sugar beat in the yolk of an egg, and, when perfectly creamy, add the white, which has been beaten to a froth, then add the water and stir it very carefully. The brandy should be beaten with the butter and sugar.

Bread Pudding.

Take a quart basinful of stale bread, and soak in two quarts of sweet milk two hours (keep in a cool place while soaking); then mash well with a spoon, and take out all the hard pieces. Beat light four eggs and stir into this, then add two teaspoonfuls of salt, a little nutmeg, and one fourth of a cup of sugar, if you serve it with sauce; if not, one and a half cupfuls. Bake three-quarters of an hour, and serve with lemon sauce. Some put raisins in, but it must be much stiffer if you have them, and the delicacy of the pudding is thereby lost.

Corn Starch Pudding.

One quart of milk, six tablespoonfuls of cornstarch, three eggs, one teaspoonful of salt. Put the milk in a basin, and set the basin into a kettle with boiling water, and when it comes to a boil stir in the cornstarch and eggs, which prepare in the following manner: Wet the cornstarch with one cup of cold milk, and then stir into it the eggs which are well beaten. After the starch is added to the boiling milk it will cook in three minutes: beat well to make smooth. Serve with sugar and cream or wine sauce. Never add the eggs after the starch has been stirred into the boiling milk; if you do the egg will be in spots in it.

CAKE.

Tea Cake.

ONE spoonful of butter, one cup of sugar, one of milk, one pint of prepared flour. Beat the sugar and butter together, and then the two eggs; next stir the milk with them, and then stir in the flour. Turn it, about an inch deep, into shallow pans, and bake in a quick oven. To be eaten warm.

Berry Cake.

Make the same as tea-cake, only pint and a half of flour, and stir in one pint of blueberries.

Plain Cup Cake.

Half a cup of butter, one of sugar, three of prepared flour, one of milk, three eggs, and lemon or nutmeg to taste. Beat the butter light, then add the sugar gradually, beating all the time until it is a cream, and then add the eggs, which have been beaten light, and the milk; mix all these well together, and then stir in the flour. Flavor and bake either in loaves or sheets; when done, the place on top where it has cracked open will look well done. If baked in loaves, it will take forty minutes; in sheets, twenty. This quantity will make two small loaves.

Soft Molasses Gingerbread, No. 2.

One cup of molasses, one teaspoonful of saleratus, one of ginger, one tablespoonful of butter or lard, a pinch of salt, if you use lard. Stir this together, and then pour on half a cup of *boiling* water, and one pint of flour. Bake about one inch deep in a sheet. This is very nice if pains are taken to have the water boiling, and to beat it well when the flour is added.

SAUCES AND DRESSINGS.

Drawn Butter.

BEAT one cup of butter and two spoonfuls of flour to a cream, and pour over this one pint of boiling water. Set on the fire, and let it come to a boil, but do *not boil*. Serve immediately.

Egg Sauce.

Chop up two hard-boiled eggs, and stir into drawn butter.

Oyster Sauce.

Set a basin on the fire with half a pint of oysters and one pint of boiling water; let them boil three minutes, and then stir in half a cup of butter beaten to a cream, with two spoonfuls of flour; let this come to a boil, and serve.

Salad Dressing.

One tablespoonful of mustard, one-half of sugar, one teaspoonful of salt, one-fourth of cayenne pepper, and the yolks of three uncooked eggs. Put this mixture in an earthen dish and set on ice; stir with a wooden or silver spoon until it is all well mixed, then add, very gradually, one bottle of table oil. Stir until very light; then stir in half a cup of vinegar. Be sure that you stir evenly, and one way all the time. This is enough for four quarts of salad.

N. B. You can use six yolks of eggs, and one-half or even one-fourth of a bottle of oil.

Boiled Salad Dressing.

Three eggs, one tablespoonful of sugar, one of oil, one each of mustard and salt, scant one cup of vinegar, one cup of milk. Beat the eggs, and add the other ingredients, then stir all together over a basin of boiling water until about as thick as soft custard. Cool and bottle.

Gentlemen will find this easily made and convenient, as it will keep one or two weeks if kept in a cool place. It takes from twelve to fifteen minutes to cook.

Caper Sauce.

Into a pint of drawn butter stir three spoonfuls of capers.

Mint Sauce.

Chop fine half a cupful of mint, and add to it a cup of vinegar and a spoonful of sugar.

Viniagrette Sauce.

One teaspoonful of white pepper, one of salt, one-half of mustard, half a cup of vinegar, one tablespoonful of oil. Mix salt, pepper, and mustard together, then *very* slowly add the vinegar, and, after all is well mixed, add the oil. To be eaten on cold meats or fish.

Tartare Sauce.

Made the same as salad dressing, with a little more vinegar and pickles cut up fine and stirred into it.

Brown Sauce.

Three tablespoonfuls of pork fat, two of flour, one pint of boiling water, salt and pepper to taste. When the fat is hot, stir in the dry flour, and cook until brown, then stir in gradually the boiling water. Season to taste, and cook five minutes. This sauce can be varied by adding any kind of catsup.

Dried Apple Sauce.

Pick and wash the apples carefully, then place in a tin pail with a cover. For one pint of dried apple, cut the thin yellow skin off a lemon, and then pare and cut up the inside. Put the yellow skin (be careful not to get any of the white) and the inside into the kettle with the apple, and three pints of cold water. Cover tight, and simmer three hours, then put in one pint of sugar, but do not stir the apple, and simmer two hours longer. *Never stir* dried apple-sauce.

DRINKS.

Tea.

Scald the teapot, and put in the tea, allowing one teaspoonful to each person; pour over this half a cup of *boiling* water (soft water is the best), and steep in a hot place, but not where it will boil, ten minutes; then turn in all the boiling water you wish, and serve.

Coffee.

For coffee, two-thirds Java and one-third Mocha gives you a very fine flavor. When buying, have them mix it in the store.

Shells.

Put one quart of cold water and half a cup of shells into the pot, and boil gently four or five hours; add boiling water occasionally. About twenty minutes before serving, add one pint of new milk and boiling water enough to make three pints in all. Let this boil a few minutes, strain and serve.

Chocolate.

With four spoonfuls of grated chocolate, mix one of sugar, and wet with one of *boiling* water. Rub this smooth with the bowl of the spoon, and then stir into one pint of boiling water; let this boil up once, and then add one pint of good milk; let this boil up once, and serve.

Prepared Cocoa.

Prepared cocoa is made the same as chocolate, omitting the sugar. All milk may be used if preferred. Never boil chocolate or prepared cocoa more than one minute. Boiling makes it oily. The quicker it is used after making the better.

Coffee, No

Half a cup of dry coffee, one egg, shell and all. Mix coffee and egg together, then pour on one quart of boiling water. Boil ten minutes, and then add half a cup of cold water; pour coffee into the cup and back again to pot. Let it stand a few minutes.

To make Mead.

One pint and a half of brown sugar, half a pint of molasses. Pour on this three pints of boiling water. Let this stand till blood warm, then add two ounces of tartaric acid and one of essence of sassafras.

When cold, bottle.

To use Mead.

Put one tablespoonful of the mead in the bottom of a glass, then fill two-thirds full of cold water, then stir in one-fourth of a teaspoonful of soda, and drink while foaming. Make mead before leaving home.

FOR THE SICK.

Rice Water for Diarrhœa.

Put one cup of rice into the frypan, and stir over the fire until it is a dark brown. If convenient, after it has been browned, pound it. Take half a cup of the rice, and pour over it nearly one quart of water, and let it stand on the stove twenty minutes; then strain, and add boiled milk and sugar to taste. Drink freely of this.

Flour Gruel.

Let one quart of fresh milk come to a boil, and then stir in one tablespoonful of flour, which has been mixed with milk enough to make a smooth paste; boil this mixture thirty minutes, being careful not to let it burn. Season with salt, and strain. The patient should be kept warm and quiet.

Oat Meal Gruel.

Into one quart of boiling water, sprinkle two tablespoonfuls of oatmeal; let this boil sixty minutes; season with salt, strain, and serve. If sugar, milk, or cream is wished, it may be added.

Indian Meal Gruel.

One quart of boiling water; stir into this one spoonful of flour and two of Indian meal, mixed with a little cold water. Boil thirty minutes. Season with salt, and strain. Use sugar and cream if you choose. If flour is not liked, use another spoonful of meal instead.

INDEX

T

V

W

Lector House believes that a society develops through a two-fold approach of continuous learning and adaptation, which is derived from the study of classic literary works spread across the historic timeline of literature records. Therefore, we aim at reviving, repairing and redeveloping all those inaccessible or damaged but historically as well as culturally important literature across subjects so that the future generations may have an opportunity to study and learn from past works to embark upon a journey of creating a better future.

This book is a result of an effort made by Lector House towards making a contribution to the preservation and repair of original ancient works which might hold historical significance to the approach of continuous learning across subjects.

HAPPY READING & LEARNING!

LECTOR HOUSE LLP
E-MAIL: lectorpublishing@gmail.com